WEST POINT

WEST POINT

Photography by Marcia Lippman

Text by James Salter

EDITION STEMMLE

Zurich New York

Its location is remote, its situation austere. Lying inland, on the heights above a great river it has—even long after the days when it was, like Vicksburg or Quebec, a cork in a bottle, a dominating stronghold—the aspects of a fortress. It sits on the high bank in isolation. The railroad does not go there any longer, the boats that once went up and down the river have disappeared. There is no convenient airport. You do not visit it casually, you must journey to it, make a pilgrimage, the last part of it as with all such places, past souvenir shops, motels, and fast-food outlets. It defies all that. It is, in many ways, a serene place, beyond the clamor of mere events. Everyone in the country has heard of it; it is a school, a military post, a former monastery, a shrine. Its alumni have held the fate of the nation in their hands.

The great river is the Hudson. The school is West Point. For two hundred years it has provided leaders of the U.S. Army and along with them an army's ethos.

It is a place dense with names, the hundreds on Battle Monument overlooking the river, those on plaques in Cullum Hall—a magnificent building donated by a devoted graduate—and the Old Cadet Chapel, the names in the sally ports—first captains going back a century and distinguished cadets—the myriad names in the cemetery—commanders of divisions, corps, armies, as well as those who died, many in war, before attaining such rank—the names in front of quarters and on doors, thousands of names, all of them a kind of humus from which the new, the yet-to-be-known names and classes rise. Some names are there only temporarily, others for all time but nearly forgotten—the names are the Corps, they are West Point, what it has been and will always be.

Something of what West Point has been and is now is caught in these pages. If you have never been there, these photographs, in both an ordinary and sometimes mythic way, will show it to you bathed in what seems to be some kind of ionic light, almost as if being seen for the last time. If you *have* been there or more, if you have gone to school there, you may find among these images one you will hold dear, as certain things said or hours passed are cherished. A photograph is a fragment of time that can become a relic, sometimes a sacred relic, even a poem. It can be glanced at for a moment and forgotten or retain a haunting power through the years, often through lifetimes, attesting to things that existed, restoring them.

In the morning, inwardly both nervous and expectant, you drive north amid the green trees and hills, following the course of the river that for the most part lies unseen though in days to come it will always be a presence. The mist rises from it on summer mornings, the gray ice clogs it in winter. The train to Albany runs on the far side of it, a train you can often hear while studying at night.

The road winds on, sun-dappled and smooth. What awaits you this July morning is known and unknown. It is a threshold, and already there is the slight uneasiness of not being able to turn back. Perhaps you are with your family. You talk to them or remain silent, not knowing why. The road descends, the trees thin out. The bridge at Bear Mountain, silver and unexpected, comes into sight.

Past the emblematic gate there is little that is imposing to be seen. West Point withholds its glamor until you have gone much further, reached its heart, but even so, in the stonework, the road, the carefully maintained rows of quarters above, there is the impression of firmness and order. A boy who once, in the winter dusk, saw the distant lights of a school set in its fields and at that moment fell in love with it and determined one day to go there—perhaps having once seen West Point you felt the same way, or it may have been from seeing a film or a brochure, perhaps even only from having heard the magical name, but on this day, with hundreds of others, the dream you have had is becoming true and you enter, unconfident and proud, a new life.

There is no counting the things of that summer, from the first day when, newly formed up, you march to the end of the Plain to take an oath, to the heat of July and August when, day after day, to a rigid schedule, you are fashioned into the semblance of a soldier and cadet. The rules to obey, procedures to follow, faces, names, responses—it comes in unending waves. This is the Honor Code. This is parade rest. That is Trophy Point. These are called trousers. Gradually, eating, running, dressing, drilling, you become part of it. The noise never ceases, the voices and cries. Around you they are no longer strangers, there's the guy who is very funny, irrepressible, another who seems well centered and strong, the one who is a bit slow, the one with the great smile, the one with a famous name, that of his father, that he wears lightly. You're not yet friends but you are in it together, women and men, and finally, together, you make it through. In later years, perhaps, you will read your early letters home with their exaggerations and homesickness, but the great free school open to all but choosing only a few is now yours.

The company is everything. Within the Corps the companies are like large families. They have their overall personality and their stars, but there is another family nearly as important and in some cases more so, in sports. Rank and class lines are erased, you are playing for Army. There are no athletic scholarships, although talent is taken into account, and those out on the field or court have no free ticket.

Great captains belong to history and appear rarely, but there are captains of teams each year, sometimes memorable, both captain and team. You will eventually forget courses, grades, weekends, everything that was so important, but all through life you remember teammates and those who excelled. Nothing, it seems, possesses greater purity. There are no grades in sports nor are you promoted, in theory, for accomplishment in them, but they inscribe their mark like nothing else and teach what no class can teach. And you need not be a national champion to know the greatest of victories: beating Navy.

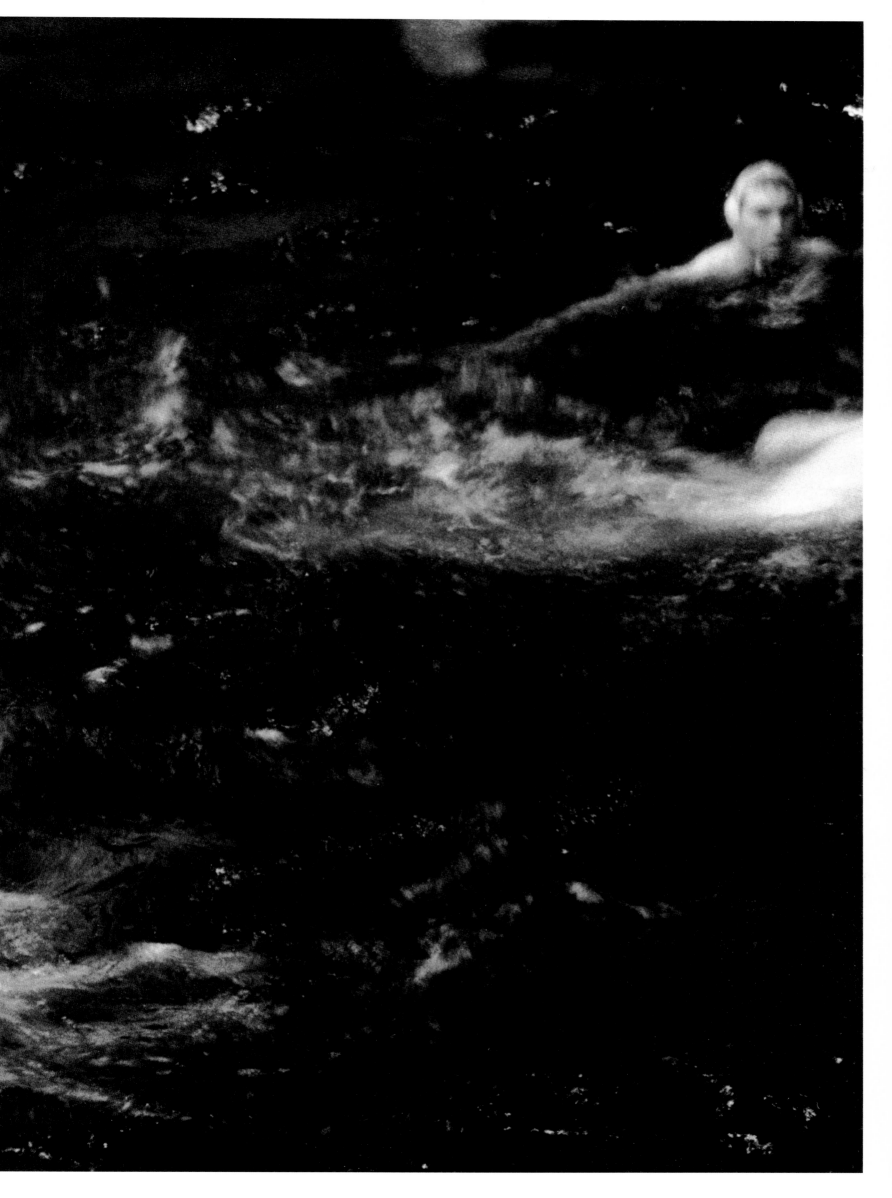

It is not all grim, far from it. There is the consoling silence of the library, there are Sunday mornings, cancelled parades, the first snow. Pizzas, impromptu parties, practical jokes. There was the very tall plebe standing in formation and the runt first classman who happened to notice him as he walked past. The first classman stops and, looking up, begins to brace him. "Pull in your chin," he says, circling round, "heave those shoulders back, stand up straight, pop your chest up, you hear me, mister?"

>Tall plebe: *(Strained voice, obeying)* Sir, may I ask a question?
>
>First classman: Go ahead.
>
>Tall plebe: Where are you, sir?

There is the joy of being out of barracks, in the field, of being tested, of working together, even of complaining and making a mental note never to do it like this when you are running things. Days of sunlight and soldiering. You have never been so hungry, so weary. *Today I have given all I have to give . . .* There is nothing greater than that. To give everything, that is what they are really teaching, to discover for yourself there is nothing you cannot do and at the same time show you how to do it. What was childhood but discovering the world? What is youth but running with the others and finding out whether you belong or not?

*J*une will come soon, lieutenants we shall be...

It has been so far off for so long, graduation, and then the last months seem to come in a rush. There are moments when you look backwards and remember when you were like those in the classes behind you, and it's true, even if some of them manage to surpass you later, they will always be younger, always behind you.

Before you lies the new life, the real one of work and duty, the life of the people, serving them. It will be gray walls, farewell; parades, inspections, exams, farewell. Keep in touch, you will say to friends, and there will be others you hardly knew who will become close as you go on to training and service together. In the army you will be the lowest of the low, the sergeants will teach you, the majors scorn you. You will go to outfits where no one seems to notice you, but on the wedding finger is your ring. It may show up in a crammed jewelry store someday or in a pawnshop, but it will always say: This is what I was.

Is West Point a club—do its graduates stick together and favor one another? They will deny it, still there are those four years and everything they meant. When you see another graduate in a unit or on a staff you know pretty well what to expect. You can dispense with the proofs. And it's strange, even those who didn't make it, failed or were kicked out, still count themselves more or less as one of the class and carry a cachet.

So the fourth summer approaches, but this one you will not have to go through, the long years are over. It was a lifetime ago when you entered. Everything that was shouted at you, all the lectures, commands, the confusion of them, the seeming senselessness, the noise, now it is clear what was really being said: Be strong, belong to something, belong to honor.

At the threshold of summer, then, belonging, you are ready to leave.

James Salter

Captions

4   General Dwight Eisenhower, The Plain

7   C.B.T. (Cadet Basic Training), The Plain,
    New Cadet

8   R-Day (Reception Day), Central Area,
    Man in the Red Sash, processing new cadet
    *R-Day is the first day of the new cadets' West
    Point experience. They are issued uniforms,
    receive haircuts, are instructed in the rudi-
    ments of drill, and end the day by taking their
    oath of office as cadets on the Plain, the
    parade ground in front of the Barracks.
    Upperclassmen supervise every aspect of this
    initiation.*

10 R-Day, Central Area, Bravo Company

11 R-Day, Scott Barracks

13 R-Day, Central Area, Men in the Red Sash,
    process new cadets

14 C.B.T., Formation, Washington Apron
    *Cadet Basic Training, commonly referred to
    as Beast Barracks, is a six-week period of
    intense military instruction that brings new
    cadets up to West Point standards. They
    receive instruction in drill, wear of the uni-
    form, basic tactics, and marksmanship, and
    they undergo physical training. The period
    ends with a week of maneuvers culminating in
    a twelve-mile road march. At the end of this
    period, during Reorganization Week, the new
    cadets are integrated into cadet companies.*

15 C.B.T., Washington Apron, Drill and Cere-
    monies

16 C.B.T., The Plain, Manual of Arms

17 C.B.T., The Plain, Cadet Officer

19 C.B.T., Trophy Point, Fame Monument,
    "They're all fickle but one."

21 C.B.T., The Plain, Drill

22 Formation, Washington Apron

23 Pep Rally, Central Area

25 C.B.T., The Plain, Drill

26 C.B.T., The Plain, Drill

27 C.B.T., The Plain, Drill

29 C.B.T., Washington Apron, Formation for
    Field Training

31 Formation, Central Area

32 Michie Stadium

Cadet Field Training takes place at Camp Buckner, a many-thousand-acre training area at West Point. For nearly eight weeks, cadets who have completed plebe year receive advanced tactical training under the leadership of upperclass cadets and with the participation of a reinforced battalion of light infantry from the Regular Army. The cadets also travel to Fort Knox, Kentucky, to receive training in armored warfare. The summer training ends in a series of ceremonies called Camp Illumination, referring to a nineteenth-century custom of dances under torchlight with colored lantern slides projected onto tent sides.

A Brief History of West Point

About fifty miles north of New York City, the Hudson River narrows and turns through an S-shaped curve cut by glaciers into granite highlands on both sides. This "West Point of the Hudson" assumed strategic importance during the Revolutionary War and became the largest garrison of the Continental army. The military post guarded a great iron chain stretched across the river to deny passage to British ships. The heavily fortified position, deemed too difficult to attack, was never tested in combat. West Point's defensive works, designed by European engineers, became the logical place to establish the United States Military Academy in 1802. Intending to educate only artillerymen and engineers, the Academy's first superintendent, Jonathan Williams, a nephew and secretary to Benjamin Franklin, looked to French military practices for inspiration; accordingly, the courses at the new school included engineering, mathematics, and physics, as well as French, the language necessary to study the most advanced military texts of the time.

Under the leadership of Sylvanus Thayer, superintendent from 1817 to 1833, the school took on much of the character that it has retained to this day. He established a four-year curriculum and expanded the heavy focus on mathematics, physics, engineering, and French. Thayer also instituted a course in moral philosophy, which included grammar, history, and geography as well. Drawing, necessary for mapmaking and engineering, was added to the curriculum at this time. Daily recitation of all cadets in all subjects became the standard pedagogical practice, one West Point still retains in some disciplines.

The first major test of this system was in the war with Mexico, 1846–48, during which junior officers Robert E. Lee, Ulysses S. Grant, Thomas J. Jackson, and many others established exemplary reputations in battle. Of the 523 Academy graduates who fought in the war, 452 were cited for gallantry in action.

West Point graduates also made substantial contributions to the nation in other areas, most notably in developing canals, railroads, bridges, lighthouses, harbors, and the like. As the country's sole engineering school until 1830, it was the only source of academically prepared engineers, and many of its graduates became professors or heads at the numerous engineering and technical colleges that were founded in the nineteenth century.

During the Civil War, approximately one-fourth of its graduates fought with the Confederacy, while the rest remained with the Union. West Point graduates commanded both sides in fifty of fifty-five major battles, and commanded one side or the other in the remaining five. Officers such as Grant, Lee, Jackson, Meade, Thomas, Sherman, Sheridan, and Halleck proved that West Point produced extraordinarily competent soldiers and leaders.

This preeminence in military leadership continued throughout the nation's wars. World War I leaders such as John J. Pershing, Douglas MacArthur, and

George Patton were Academy graduates; thirty-four of thirty-eight corps and division commanders were also from West Point. Many World War I-era cadets rose to prominence in World War II: Dwight Eisenhower, Omar Bradley, Anthony McAuliffe, Maxwell Taylor, and hundreds of others. Similarly, many of the Army leaders in the Korean and Vietnam wars, such as James Van Fleet, William Westmoreland, and Creighton Abrams, were West Point graduates, as was Norman Schwarzkopf, leader of the allied coalition during Desert Storm.

Currently, the Corps of Cadets consists of about 4,000 men and women (admitted since 1976 and now comprising about 15 percent of the total), drawn from every state in the United States and numerous foreign countries. They undergo a rigorous series of military training exercises in the summers, beginning the summer before their freshman year, and complete a core curriculum of about thirty courses, balanced among mathematics, science, engineering, humanities, and public affairs; in addition, cadets take eight to twelve courses in one of over fifty majors or fields of study. They undergo a comprehensive physical development program of intramurals, individual sports, and intercollegiate competition, along with physical education classes, throughout their four years. Active Army officers compose about 80 percent of the faculty; the rest are civilians, all of whom hold doctorates in their fields. West Point graduates must serve five years on active duty after graduation.

In the years prior to the Civil War, West Point Superintendent Richard Delafield (1838-45; 1856-61) began increasing the size and quality of the classrooms, barracks, and other buildings, adopting what he called a "military" or "Tudor" Gothic architectural style, a practice followed still. The battlements, turrets, and mullioned windows make West Point appear as something out of a romance, emphasizing what Henry James called its "native nobleness of position." Some very distinguished American architects have been inspired by this setting to leave their mark on West Point, including Richard Morris Hunt (Pershing Barracks), Stanford White (Cullum Hall, Battle Monument, the West Point Club), and, most notably, Ralph Adams Cram and Bertram Goodhue (Cadet Chapel, Thayer Hall, Taylor Hall, quarters, barracks, stables, and other facilities). Their 1903-10 revitalization of the Academy, in conjunction with its centennial, formed the campus plan that we see today. They retained the tradition of using stone quarried from the Academy's grounds for their buildings, making it appear as if they rise naturally out of the very land on which they sit. This rooted sense of place creates and sustains the notions of "Duty, Honor, Country" that have marked West Point and its graduates for two hundred years.

Michael Burke

A graduate of the Virginia Military Institute, Lieutenant Colonel Michael Burke (U.S. Army, retired) taught English for eight years at West Point. He served in the First Armored Division during the Gulf War.

In 1986, The New York Foundation for the Arts Artist in Residency program and the Cadet Fine Arts Forum made my initial stay at The United States Military Academy possible. I offer my heartfelt thanks to the many extraordinary people who inspired and supported my work at West Point during that year, and who contributed greatly to the evolution of this book: Lieutenant General Dave Palmer, Superintendent; Brigadier General Peter Boylan, Commandant of Cadets; Brigadier General Roy Flint, Dean of the Academic Board; Mr. Carl Ullrich, Director of Intercollegiate Athletics; the inspirational Department of English, in particular Colonel Peter Stromberg, Colonel Jack Capps, Lieutenant Colonel Terence Freeman, Captain David Tippett, and my co-teacher and friend Major Wally Bransford; Major Rod Morgan; and the entire Corps of Cadets at West Point. Additional thanks, for their assistance in the final preparation of this book, to Retired Colonel Seth Hudgins, President of the Association of Graduates; Retired Lieutenant Colonel Michael Burke; and Andrea Hamburger, Public Affairs Office at West Point.

My special thanks to James Salter for gracing my pictures with his words.

I salute you all!

Marcia Lippman

Editorial Direction by Joan L. Brookbank
and Marion Elmer
Layout and Typography by Giorgio Chiappa, Zurich
Lithography by Seelitho AG, Arbon, Switzerland
Printed and bound by Grafiche Duegi,
San Martino B.A. (Verona), Italy

ISBN 3-908163-50-1

With the ISBN 3-908163-75-7, a special edition of
West Point has been printed in a limited number.
The special edition contains an original print, num-
bered and signed by the artist.